Zmagria

POEMS

Mouna Ammar

Fifth Avenue Press is a locally focused and publicly owned publishing imprint of the Ann Arbor District Library. It is dedicated to supporting the local writing community by promoting the production of original fiction, nonfiction, and poetry written for children, teens, and adults.

Printed in the United States of America

First Printing 2024

Book and Cover Design by Nathaniel Roy
Edited by Zilka Joseph

ISBN: 978-1-956697-30-8 (Paperback)

Fifth Avenue Press
343 S. Fifth Ave
Ann Arbor, MI 48104
fifthavenue.press

In the name of Allah, all things begin.

To my mother, my father, and each one of my siblings for being my everythings.

To my Mehdi – my sunshine now and always.

To my beloved teachers: Sister Haleema Mu'min (upon her soul be mercy) & Sister Karen Pradia for modeling the best of what I hope to be.

To my DC hermanas & amigas who believed in me from day one.

To my Wolf Pack who run with me.

To Leila and Mari who held space time and again over the years.

To Uzma who magically wrote along.

To Brother Yoshi who mentored and exemplified a life of creative spirit.

To LuFuki & Divine Providence who walked the way.

To Said – whose greatest surprise is that he married a writer.

Zmagria:

The word zmagria is slang in North African Arabic- Moroccan, Algerian- for an immigrant or someone who immigrated; zmagri (masculine) or zmagria (feminine). I didn't know about this word until adulthood and was shocked to find out that there was a label for me by people of my same cultural and ethnic background. While it isn't used in a derogatory way, I have certainly heard it used to identify those in the diaspora as a somewhat diluted status of Moroccan or Algerian or Tunisian. I decided to own the word and the notion of being the hybrid not-easily-defined "outsider insider" and make it a source from which to draw strength. I also just like the way it sounds!

Contents

Poetry and beauty are always making peace. When you read something beautiful you find coexistence; it breaks walls down.

—Mahmoud Darwish

Invocation

Breath.
Return
to me
from wherever
in these traveling limbs
 you scurried to hide
or catch your own quiet repose.

Breath.
Disperse
through thousands
of traveling veins inside.
Glide
back to my face, my embrace

Let me inhale.

I.

VERMONT Ave.

To Vermont Ave. we went
buying our *verduras*
Walking down
cracked sidewalks
to a soundtrack of rap, norteñas, soul, *mariachi*
We took care of weekly chores at the *lavandería*
Scrunched our noses
at the sharp singing aromas from scarred woks
hidden in deep kitchens.
Botanicas saw us along home.

On Vermont Ave.
We prayed early community prayers
In a low-ceiling hall exactly the size and color and shade
Today — as the day it opened.
This is edgy for a city where nothing lasts past
a moment's trends
On brand though for a practice
as timeless as prayer
as healing as momentary motionlessness.

There,
We memorized our first few short verses of the Qur'an
Reading them out in girl-pitched unison
and then one by one by one
We hurried back to our multi-language parents
to recite proudly out loud again
Feeling that was a thing learned, done,
dusted and trusted to memory.
Now we try to dust off again.

Vermont Ave. we listened
to bullets fly
sirens whine
and the forgotten homeless
shaking their dusty foam cups for dimes
off the highway exit ramps
Wondering when they would find
their way to our door.

Vermont.
We turned left of it and found our book-free learning
old museums.
We turned right to pick up letters *par avion*
notes marking seasons
Each corner exhaling the smoke of decisions
Milestones
Busy uncertainties.

On it
were the bleeding clots
of street corner crews
Sharp-dressed reporters for the six o'clock news
Mostly lacking real clues
and holding The Call was the old story guy
in a bow tie selling the best bean pies.

There
the Exposition train used to click clack past
whistling
conductor waving
Now it's a light rail — old lines sunk deep
in the forehead of the intersection
buried under sleek pavement
and spindly landscaping.

Choppers woke me up middle of the night
to America's dreams and nightmares
Across the street
a place of higher learning sealed from poor scholars
offering only stares.
Every gated entry suffocated by
an arm and a guard — swollen meanings.

It
is where I go to reunite shreds of boxed childhood memories.
Knowing too well that whatever I'm looking for cannot
will not
ever be the same as back then.
The past shows up once —
And mom's dreams —
deferred
Dad's dreams —
Blurred.
Ours continue
to live
and stir.

Bandage for my Day

I washed as I usually do, hastily
Flipping through my domineering mental to-do list
didn't remove my watch.
My favorite part to splash was my face
the edges along my ears.
The cold water woke me up
from the deep sleep of hurry.
The phone rang frenzied at exactly the same moment
of course.
Kiddo lost it over
a toy that wouldn't cooperate and needed attention-
that same moment too.
And someone knocked at the door
Also that exact moment
asking if I could talk — just a few minutes of your time-
about my vote in the upcoming election.
The grumbly trash truck rolled by reminding me
that I did not discard the tied-up bag by the garage door
from the night before.
The mundane sliced my day into uneven pieces
And then
I glanced over
my thinned rectangular emerald and white velvet rug returned
the glance
stretched out
not a single wrinkle
on the ground
at a correct angle.
Suddenly it reminded me
of a bandage I once placed over a gash
on my knees
that let me keep
running.

THE SOUND OF JUDGING

She's stuck up.

She's so sweet.

She's holy.

She's holier-than-thou.

She's hypocritical.

She's pure.

She's way too devout.

She's way too repressed.

She's unapproachable, man.

Maaaan, she's exotic!

"She's tha good geyrr whoo cuffer she will be tha good wife foorr my sun."

She's too traditional.

She's — I wonder where she's from - probably from the middle east.

She's not American.

She's not covering right.

She takes this covering shit way too literally.

She's brainwashed.

She's too independent.

She's a victim of patriarchy.

She's escaping reality.

She needs to lighten up.

She probably has a limited education.

She's SO ARTICULATE!!

She's too much of a nonconformist.

She's too much of a conformist.

Does she have to rub it in?

Does she have to be so secretive?

May Allah guide her, doesn't she know her wrist is showing?

She's SOOO unique!

She's just fixated on this modesty trend.

She's not her own person.

She must not speak English.

She must be Arab.

She's not all that Arab.

She must be Iranian.

Where's she from, Afghanistan?

She must be a terrorist.

She must be a terrorist's/extremist's wife. Daughter. No. Wife.

She's probably not comfortable with her voice.

She must be shy. Timid, Timid. That's it.

She must be married.

She must be a nun.

She must be miserable.

Charge her 90, ya sabes, tienen plata.

Doesn't she realize she's in a country where women are free?!

She just doesn't have the body to flaunt.

She doesn't know her human rights.

She must be hot under that.

She must be lying about it being so normal.

She's probably gonna have an arranged marriage.

She into hiphop?

Wait. She rhymes?

Does she know that the DEI position is open?

She writes?!

Her skills aren't exactly what our company is seeking at the moment.

We gained a clearer idea of our focus in hiring a candidate.

I can't talk to her she'll be critical of me.

She'll just think I'm a bad Muslim.

She'll think I'm a sinner.

She'll judge me.

She'll judge

Me

She'll

Judge.

ID

My name is not a bridge.
No.
No bulging, straining, stepped on, near swaying
under the weight of heedless travelers'
footsteps upon frantic footfalls.
No bridge here.
No suspended arms slung so far out of their sockets
Dislocated.
No bridge here, fixed in architectural silence.

Think of my name as an ornate doorway
carved threshold — bold in color
intricate in texture.
Stand in front of me full-handed
requesting permission
to be welcomed in
And then do as a true guest would.
Cherish the company.
Thank your host.
Do not take up too much time.
Extend your own invitation.

هوية

إسمي ليس جسر للعابرين
لا
إسمي ليس معبر تحت أقدام المارين
واعباء المسافرين
وهيجان المسرعين.
ذراعَي ليست معلقة
بنيتي ليست صامتة.
لا.
هويتي ليست ممر
للحائرين.
اعتبروا إسمي بوابة مزخرفة
جذابة الألوان
متقنة القوام
حافظة لمسكن الأحلام
قفوا أمام اسمي واطرقوا بوابته
كالضيوف الكرام.

Finding Me

So many little parts and tinier pieces of parts
hurtled onto my lap one day – their force knocking me down
my goosebumps heavy as a sandbag.
These imperfectly chiseled pieces.
That were previously discarded but only to a dusty
somewhere of a room
– not disposed of –
A spilled jigsaw
Bits scattered everywhere.
The weight of all the fragments was more than I could carry
and all I decided to hold.

To My Habibi

The late Ramadan pre-dawn moment you appeared
outside of my body
in that strangely long cavernous hospital room
that held us both and
I asked them to keep barely lit
                        — Entering the world offered a light of its own —
I wondered for that spellbound second
If you were
an apparition or a vision
In that suspended moment
my soul
Spun upon
the gasping realization that
it was actually possible
to breathe
when split
in half.

Time-travel

I time travel a lot but
not to a time
To a memory of times –
sugar dusted images I keep visiting because
That's easier than loving my now
though I try.
Time travel to neighborhoods that raised me
to the beat of
MJ & Anita Baker
Stevie & Chente
The neighborhoods of casual low chain link fences
soft-edged one-story bungalows with welcoming red tile roofs.

Maybe it's a trip to the non-stop roaring hum
of cross-stitched freeways
flowing along the long cruisin'
Artesia, Imperial, and frowning Rosecrans.

Funny how
none of the images include the sting
of not ever being able to afford tickets to a Laker's game
Nor one of the latest cars everyone drove –
Nor a fabled hacienda on a palm-lined drive
Only the silent cast-down look on my father's face
after spending the bigger portion of his days
battling expenses
trying to shorten
the endless drives
of not moving- just inching
As the voice of Egypt's legend Abdul Basit
kept him
himself.

My All-American Car – A Story

My first car.
Hefty all-American 1997 Mercury Grand Marquis.
It was a used car – a gift I never expected.
Some might call it a starter car.
Maybe starter car conjures zippy small thing.
Not this automobile.
This was a lux battleship of a vehicle
or as my sibs and I called it, our gangster car, the tank.
We LOVED it. It could fit all five of us and our mountain of stuff for an
impromptu trek to the beach or a hike.
It was an eight-cylinder ship floating down southern California's infamous
web of freeways.
I could have in no way bought it for myself at the time.
White with a leather gray-blue interior. A cruiser.

It originally belonged to the late parents of my friend Samia.
Still can't say "late" when I say her name.
She was Lebanese and older than me by about 17 years or so. She was
everything I was not and I was a lot of things she was not.
She was chic and pretty. I was homely. I may have been book smart but she
was all kinds of life smart. I was about reading the writing and she was all
about reading the world. She- a socialite in glamorous circles in New York,
California, London, Egypt, Beirut, the Persian gulf, and a lot of other places in
between. I was a homeschooled gal from Inglewood and Long Beach and Mar
Vista with friends I could count on one hand at the time.
You could smell the greatest designer fragrances when she passed by.
I was the aroma of my mom's home cooking, and some deep old country
soaps.
We were the different faces of the same priceless Arab coin.

All I knew were the working folk areas of LA from the early weeks of my life
Wore old school clothes and shoes (think lots of browns, cottons, blouses,
closed toed formal).

Samia? She wore European brand name trends, fashion styles, Jackie 'O
sunglasses. She had that Santa Monica glamor and fresh vibe. I had that
neighborhood girl groove.
She traveled the world. I commuted from home to campus to the mosque to
the library, to the Arabic shop, and back.
She was a successful businesswoman — entrepreneurial par excellence. I was
solid pounded worker-bee material.

The contrasts were like fuel now that I think about it.
But
Do you grasp how different and how unlikely it was that we became friends?
Those make some of the most eternal and meaningful friendships. We
met somehow when she was looking for an Arabic tutor who would teach
her only child Arabic and Qur'an. At the time, I was a green grad student,
hesitantly looking for tutoring jobs. Her son — shaggy jet black hair and
mischievous witty 9-year old taught
me
more
than
I ever taught
him.

The tutoring visits over a couple of years became friendship through Qur'an
and Arabic which we both adored
until cancer
snatched her away from all of us in her young '40s.
I remember exactly where I was and how hollowed out I felt that day.

Some weeks or maybe months later — her brother reached out to me. My sister
would have wanted you to have it, he said.
And I, who speaks three languages, and reads four
had no language to offer in response to thank him. Only tears.

Our friendship extended through that car- powered by the love of sincerity.

Samia's parent's car offered connection, abundance, journeys too- of course. I clung to it even as it gave me warning sign after screaming mechanical warning sign of giving out. It was more than a set of wheels. When I drove it, it made me feel like Samia was still there, still crinkling her nose in that high-pitched sparkling giggle of hers. It also made me feel invincible. IN. VIN. CI. BLE. Ask my youngest sister. I talked back to a cop who pulled me over for speeding. In lily-ass Irvine. And miraculously got away with it. With a happy birthday wish. From a cop. We do not mess with cops in my part of SoCal.

Our friendship story is as timeless and as much a lore as a Ford manufactured car is to Americana. The romantic open road of life threw us together in precise happenstance, and we rolled with it.

I reminisce, I marvel at how her brother might have ever got the idea that Samia wanted to give me the car. Of course, she knew I did not have a car of my own but I never asked her to help me find a car. That was the kind of asking I had no clue how to think up, let alone put into words. But it was like this- our story friendship. We were both keenly perceptive about each other's needs and sensitive enough to offer support without opening old wounds or creating new ones. She needed to learn how to pray at one point and so I showed her on a visit here and a washing there. Soon she led the way to the holy cities of Makkah & Madinah, where I still yearn to go. We were kindred souls who sought out goodness and believed in it unfailingly in the midst of all kinds of ugliness we both faced at the time.

Our fairytale-like belief in goodness seems to me now like that strong vehicle- one that offered us safe and comfortable carriage

through every experience
and an engine of resilience through our ambient hills and valleys.

That Mercury Grand Marquis made for some of our most hilarious memories,
and some of our most painful losses. Samia drove that grand vehicle a good
long while after her parents died. It was her mother's after all.
She drove it for years holding on to them as long as she could with everything
she had. I followed suit.

That grand vehicle saw me drift away from a good man who couldn't fight his
demons hard enough.
That grand automobile took me to get hooded for my PhD.
That grand car sat with me at the top of Signal Hill wondering the bigger
wonderings we all have from time to time.

A lot of my memories from that period of life have disappeared
so I do not remember when or how my cruiser and I eventually parted ways.
I do not want to retrieve that memory.

All I want to remember is my gratitude for it, and for my friend Samia, her
family, her son
and our friendship.

All I want to remember is how tough that car made me feel and the paths we
shared together.
Emotions push their way out of me any time I happen to spot a car like that
on the road, and here in Michigan- the land of Ford legends- it's hard not to
catch sight of one, now and then, and smile.

If this reads as too sentimental thank the all-American automobile, thank my
friend,
Samia.

Stillness is Resilience

Here I am
Still.
I am the stripped woods and chilled waters
crisp reeds and all the ready bare twigs.
Arriving right on time
ripened dry to the song of summering jays
bright blue and violet summer flavors.
I am here and remain
under these stiff gold and gray reeds
color-fading bending stalks
that speak to me of pauses and continuings.
In my questioning acceptance and through my story
decay and birth
take their respectful cycles.
I will be here too
when the merciful snow cloaks me.

II.

1 Zmagria Place

It's my address.
They call the ones of us outside the old country
"zmagri" or "zmagria".
Like an angry epithet baring
its teeth against a wretched clenched history.

If only the ones who never experienced transplanting
knew – glimpsed
what it does-
to be yanked out
without warning and ordered to re-grow.
If only the ones who have learned
to grow transplanted– could glimpse
What it does
to run in place.

So this is one zmagria's epithet-taking.

When we returned to the States by plane back
during that heavy summer
I did not know my mother's hollow pang
but I felt it in her smile's ghost.
I heard it when she sang
her own language's melodies.
I smelled it when she baked
her mother's semolina bread
Scored slowly, decoratively
with a deliberate sharp tool
Women's memory.

A photo pale brown-orange fading
shows off my neatly swaddled
3-week-old howl in my mother's arms
Her gaunt face staring down
at me in the airplane aisle seat
She was tear-less and mournful
like the statue of the grief-stricken Madonna.

Two weeks before that inevitable journey
Metal prongs extracted me
out
from her and it took terrifying
slow
heartbeats for us to resume
inhaling and exhaling in order.
The elders bathed me
in ancestral olive oil
and did not wash it off.

Now
My own womb
Dissected in a lab
in one of the hospitals
of old America
instructs me to heal
for us both

Azulejos of my Grandmother's Hallway

Walking into my grandmother's apartment
Mustard yellow, off-white, and mocha brown tiles in patterns
sprayed the sides of the long entry hall
That space always echoed weird.

My memory hasn't kept much
But
I can hear her sharp command now in wide voweled Algerois Arabic —
Close that refrigerator door!
As if it were a portal that would somehow
snatch us away from her back to far-away America.
Our ways with food were too much for her.
We snacked endlessly.
She ate two meals a day
and drank three demi-tasse cups of fresh hand-ground black coffee
to time her day: morning, afternoon, and night.

Mama repeated the command
softening it with her explanations of her mother's ways.
In Algeria — striding to the fridge did not mean
An open chat with your bored belly.
It meant disrespect to your host — who is feeding you.
But we couldn't get that.
We were ravenous in our mother's childhood home —
Where she once hungered too
But not for food.
In Algeria, the real stash of treats hid under lock and key
in a solid dark wooden china cabinet.
There, a pot of sablés no patisserie could rival.
Ready to entertain the typically impromptu afternoon visitor-guests.
But weren't we guests too, we challenged?
No one had time to consider an answer.

Her entry hallway hosted a formal space
just as much as her grand dinner table —
For goodbyes, welcomes, brief catch-ups,
shopping arguments, introductions, snatches of gossip,
laughter and shouts, crowds greeting and mourning,
indirect askings and parallel furtive answerings.
All these unfolded to the tune of
A chortling, immortal, stovetop *cafetiere*
releasing its moody full-bodied perfume
even when it was cool to the touch — which was rare.

That '60s color motif in the tiles swallowed light
except during the fading day's afternoon hours
where everything glowed golden for the together time *gouté* with viennoiseries
from the happy bakery downstairs.
Opening the door of remembering to grandma's place
squeezes my calf muscles and lungs
As if I'm climbing up the endless steep five flights of stone stairs
to her apartment again —
The dark stairwell where
every footstep created mocking acoustics
greeting the wide dark brown wooden door that she never locked
into that hallowed tiled entryway
Funny how none of the water shortages
or endless stream of visitors
take up the same room
in my memory as that ugly faded tile hallway
where everyone fought
for space.

In a Moroccan Riad

A honey moonlight
hovered far above my small black olive Kabyle eyes
which questioned and recognized.
It drew my gaze upward
in neck-bending visions of passed-down fables I memorized
but could not reach-
Outlining tangled wooden lattices- it spiraled high.
Whispers exposed themselves as arrogant echoes
Cloistered cushioned spaces concealed themselves
behind their guardian tall curtains
Which were thrown open to the bewitching evening's twin sorceresses
night air and sparkling skies.
I looked for a way
as pearl-colored pillars melted into marble hallways
Each step circled into tight archways,
Thick doorways which confronted
narrow winding stairwells that snatched
Up every breath I could spare.
The rough paintings stared at me
as I escaped deeper into the riad's heights.
It took all my careless curiosity to climb to the topmost terrace
and there at last met the moon alone
It was not enough for me to contemplate its gentle gaze
from the courtyard below
among the reclining plants and yawning fountain.
I had to ascend to
where it shone brightest —
in loving danger
like a risk-obsessed artist.

For Every Khala

Without her pretend frown

no barometer holds me accountable to my better self

Without her epic *basboosa* , *mana'eesh*, *ful*, *kaa'k*, *kofta*

no delicious memories

Without her stop-still-in-your-tracks, "NA'AM?!"

no near escapes from certain disasters and whims

Without her *"ihki bil-'arabi!"*

No childhood stories I could write from the left or the right

Without her accented comeback to rude clerks

no design of self-respect or self-knowledge

Without her anger

no reminders of what we cared about most

Without her loyalty

no one to take care of my siblings and me at the drop

of a life emergency

Without her *"yallah ya habibti"*

no sense of a harboring warmth in the thick of a scary world

Without her energy —

no community.

no Friday potluck dinners, no masjid fundraisers, no *iftars*, no weddings, no craft fairs, no talent shows or cookouts, no camps, no visits with the local church

Without her looooong *zaghrouta*

no idea how to defy tragedy and remember our peoples' dances.

Without the way she glided along a at whoever shouted a "Go back where you came from!" — no model for how to be a woman in one's own right.

Without her *thobe* and gold bracelets, head wrap, turquoise rings

no taste for the finer stuff of life

from the Maghreb to the Silk Road and all in between.

Without her palms cupped open to the sky

no compass towards that

which matters above all.

لولا خالة

لم أطمح أن أقيس ذاتي بنموذج حميد
لولا عطفها المتنكر بعبساتها الضاحكة

لم أجد في ذكرياتي أي لذة من قديم أو جديد
لولا بسبوستها وبريانيها ومناقيشها وكعكاتها وفولها ويبرأها وشوربتها وطاجينها

لم أحصل على روايات قابلة للتخليد
لولا حرصها الدائم بكلمتين لا تُنسى: "احكي بالعربي!"
لم أعرف غلاوة التنهيد
لولا وقفتها المتحدية في وجه الشامتين الشاتمين بـ"ارجعي من وين ما جيتي"

لم أصبر على بعد القريب وأدرك قرب البعيد
لولا مشاركتها لنا في صدمات الحياة

لم أرى مثالاً للصمود الصنديد
لولا زغروتتها العريقة ورقصاتها السخية للترحيب بيوم القرح أو يوم الفرح سواء

لم أفقه قوة التضامن العربي الفريد
لولا حفلاتها ومخيماتها ومعارضها للفنون ومسابقاتها الثقافية ونزهاتها الشهرية وزياراتها لمن جاورنا من كنيسة أو متحف وأنشطتها المستمرة

والله لها حق علينا مجيد
بدعائها قبل كل شيء
لأن لولا كفيها الممتدة للسماوات لما سمونا بمسارنا كعرب وأمريكان
والتاريخ لها شهيد

Ode to Ammou

When Arabic speakers call a dude "Ammou" (Uncle)
that is NO pejorative.
The title of "Ammou" is so solid in Arab cultures it is practically scripture.
If you can say "Ammou" without emotions spilling out of you, you probably
don't know what "Ammou" really means for an Arab or Arab-ish kid.
"Ammou"?
He's the one who spells out directions even when he won't stop to ask for
directions himself. They made these maps for what? He asks you, folding
them out wide in front of the window.
Dicoration?
"Ammou" is someone you go to with your troubles when your dad won't hear
sense, and "Ammou" can knock sense into your head when you, on the other
hand, won't see sense or won't do what you know you gotta do.
"Ammou" is belly laughs even if he's skinny- he's almost never skinny- and
stiff competition when arguing a point.
"Ammou" has skills.
He can grill
better than George Foreman and the Weber company put together.
drive like
he never left the old country
and sing like
that old country is right there in the supermarket aisle - during peak shopping hours.
"Ammou" wears those chunky thick wide face watches
teaches you the proper way to drink Turkish coffee or mint tea after a meal.
"Ammou" is plain 'ol bullet-proof caring
especially when you scrape your knee in front of your cool friends and need
to bury your head somewhere for that cry you don't know what to do with.
He lets you cry it out, hands you one of those lost in his pockets strawberry-
wrapped candies, then sends you to do a chore you detest just so he makes
120% sure you're feeling better.
"Ammou" has kids who might as well be your own blood siblings. You don't
realize you're not one of his own until adulting enters rude and strange.
"Ammou" knows when you broke your mom's heart and makes damn sure

you apologize

on your knees.

"Ammou" looks at you when you've messed up and somehow you wind up realizing you are way better than that.

"Ammou" is hard work, no frills, "do-what-it-takes", sharp '70s dressing, cologne that makes the walls themselves remember who passed by, and a 100%-guaranteed solution for hair loss that embarrasses only his kids and you.

Very few things are impossible for "Ammou."

He walks into a fancy store for the first time and walks out having made friends with the manager and a couple of the staff and a discount on top- a discount on something no one would have ever thought to negotiate.

He's an entrepreneur when he needs to be, a handyman when something breaks down, a therapist when you just need to think out loud. He'd have you thinking he's the neighborhood butcher on Eid.

You beat up your first car in an accident? Ammou knows a bodyshop that'll fix it without taking your payment.

"Ammou" yells at the tv as if the soccer player can hear him and "shush shush shush"'s the air itself when he sees a story of his country on the news.

"Ammou" tries to set you up with that random boy or sweet girl no matter how many times you plead with him not to. You won't stay single on his watch or prayers.

"Ammou" has seen the ugly parts of "the system" over there and over here and has a mosque to show for it — a mosque with only cold water in the bathrooms but daily overflowing parking and a little lake of shoes outside the front of the door because the community gatherings are

that good.

"Ammou" will cry when you graduate and tell you the best joke while he's in the hospital.

"Ammou" was not "Ammou" without "Khaala", and he knew she was everything.

Survivor's Instinct

This waking up every other few hours to check and respond

Feels—

This

eyes flying necessary wide open

Body held totally still at attention

Every sense

On highest alert

For noticing

Even through a screen

a hint of life

amidst the droning noises

For witnessing along

the minutest to the widest signs of

making it

seems

familiar—necessary familiar to my mother instincts

weary willing as they are.

11:08 PM dear God they're so hungry…jump

12:44 AM Doesn't anyone else hear them?

12:52 – I think they might be resting

1:30 AM

Are they covered or cold?

3:47 AM – please, are they?

Let them be breathing

Please.

5:17 AM They can't rest if they can't get clean.

7:00 AM

Anguish and relief scissor through my deepest at first light of day.

If we mother Palestine

Stand at attention

throughout the longest nights

Might she

survive?

May she grow.

My North Africans

MY SUDANESE

I am in awe of my Sudanese

They speak of everyone's good qualities first and foremost — even ones we eyebrow-raise at

They remind our inner critic to throw stones at our own glass house first.

MY TUNISIANS

I am in awe of my Tunisians

Who marry excellence and understatement

They understand beauty needs a dose of furtive humility

In order to make it in this world.

MY MOROCCANS

I am in awe of my Moroccans

Neighbors and guardians of history and grand-carved hospitality

They inhabit imagination in real time

in breathing colors and flavor.

MY LIBYANS

I am in awe of my Libyans

They let out the loudest ululations when the first news of grief reaches them.

They command our sadness to dance to God's will.

MY EGYPTIANS

I am in awe of my Egyptians

They laugh through every step of life's endurance parade

They pat our hardships on the head as if to say

"sit down little one, we've been around longer."

Couscous to Me

I do not have thousands of dollars to travel to my relatives' and ancestors'
burial grounds
along the sashaying Mediterranean coasts
lining the protective Djurdjura mountains
sailing by the wise and generous dunes of the open Sahara.
that I have heard, watched, and read so much about.
All I have is a large earthen-colored platter that
reminds me of where we all come from
heaped with steam spiraling golden grains
topped with warming root vegetables and sweet squashes that I learned to cook
using my personal Ras AlHanout blend of roasted love, pounded longing &
powdered frustration.
Couscous shares so many flavors of stories.
It offers a sacred personal ticket
my savory boarding pass
my exhausting, full, and filling journey
to everything home.

Permission

Go on.
Take up beautiful space.
Do not shrink
within.
Your essence — no way an error
needing to hide
It needs to believe in its own size.

Listen sis,
Trust the journey.
On another level and inviting plane
You have already taken off
and know your direction.
Gaze deeply
into your heart's topographies.
Do not avoid your headwinds.

Take up room

Take up the space you intend.

The room and place you need

and were already offered when you

Were granted

Your own limbs

Your own soul

Your own smile —

Your own broken

and soldered together heart —

the *you*, you have right now

Not the you

put on

through the ugliest of forces?

Or desperation

Self-loathing

or

coercion

or by the pressure to just

fit

in.

Arabic Belongs to Us All

Done.
Done being tired of hearing—when I open my mouth
that Algerians, Moroccans, Tunisians "don't speak Arabic".
We are the self-driving cars of language —
We have and have had
agile ways
with words and pronunciations.
Please keep up.

Done.
Done with this tribal possessiveness of floral tongues.
As if Arabic only belongs to one group or another.
It belongs to us all
This fluid script.

Iraqis do not own it.
Nor do the Egyptians.
The Levantines certainly don't.
The Gulfies do not either.
Though maybe the Yemenis did to some extent
Maybe the Mauritanians still do.

The notes of all the Arabics together
A full orchestra
As long as the musicians recognize
And value
That their sounds can only harmonize
With
The rolling rhythms of Arabics from
Sudan and Chad
Libya and Tunisia
Algeria and Morocco
Malta.
Hybrid sounds create
the most lasting symphonies.

III.

When I see the Suffering of My People

It steadies me to witness the way
this river's broad shoulders do not shy away
from the weight of piled snow.
It courses on holding court with the willing submerged assembly
of tree roots.
It honors seasons' changes.
Swirling in royal silence –
It rules by self-possessed murmur
And the acres it passes
heel.

In a Fancy Supermarket

In the middle of the neatest feng-shui'ed produce aisles
Arranged with spacious welcoming designer flooring and just-so lighting
that keeps you lingering longering gazing over and over
at the curated shelves - a comestibles gallery
Standing there soothed by the perfectly climate-controlled air —
I hear a younger woman's voice complaining that there were no raspberries left
during the deep freeze of
a Midwest February.
In that same instant her voice seemed to summon the image of a shabby wide-
eyed child in front of my face
The mental snapshot of that child just outside a crude mud-streaked tent
flashes in front of me
 blinding me for a true moment — an honest apparition.
For a second all I can see are those haunting dark-ringed gaping round eyes
staring off into this whole flooded with food place
piercing the falsetto of consumer complaints.
No time to ask what triggered that image's sudden visit.
The cashier glances at me saying something I cannot hear.
The mourning basket and restrained vegetables
offend the spotless floor as I attack the insides of my crossbody for a tissue
and run, escaping the dazzlingly comfortable shop.
The little basket got too heavy for my hands.
and I could not eat during a flashback from a massacre
I watched from my kitchen.

The Meaning of Unpacking

I started by saying,
I have moved so many times.
Filling and emptying boxes and making order out of pieces.

The unpacking takes careful tiptoe-ing, tripping and trying,
Failing, and daily doing.
At least this is what the therapist said,
and of course some dusting off and away and lifting
Mostly, it takes time and enough light
And being ok with having nothing for a little while.

So study your emotions – I learned
like a convinced archaeologist would approach a dig.
Treat the hint of feelings like brittle old tiles
that collapsed over a dusty forgotten story
concealing a lapiz lode of heart.
Use delicately covered fingertips,
Gentle, slow
brush strokes-
Soft, tender storing
to keep the traces of buried experiences
Intact. Observable. Resembling whole.

I did not dare tell my therapist
That I had no room to keep any relics anymore.
That I was holding onto my parents' and mine.
So I nodded and did what I could
Wondering how I'd care for
the excavated artifacts
of discovering myself.

Our Names

What portrait will the name
Yahyaoui
Sketch
On your mind and heart's canvases?

As I sat in that crowded consular office
the aromatic flow of names
emerged first in a trickle then a gush
melodius syllables
singing out so many "once upon a times"
From the quiet dark file drawers of imagination

Benzarga
Salhi
Ait Houcine
Rebbouh
Boulila
Shibli
Belqadi
Djermoun
Zemmour
BenLila
Mana
BouZidi
Khoudja
Karimi
BelQassem
Tahraoui
Azizi
Belqaid
Zerrouqi
BenYamina

A full summer bouquet
a swaying fruit orchard
sprawled out as far as the eye could see
heavy with a whole collection of fresh fruits
ripe and overflowing around crumbling old columns
Ruins and abundance together.

The names of my people's children
Caravan through time
slowly and steadily
Defying the sinking destruction
Occupation tried to offer.

In a stark but mercifully bustling office waiting area
these names move about defying
windy bureaucracies
with their cadences.
If they were kites
these names would be sailing high
above the worry-laden crowd
flouting many a drunk bet
that they'd fall fast.

If these names were a flame
They would melt red tape.
And the wrinkled men in stale ties
Would finally
Sit down.

Inheritance

I arrived into this fresh present day
this silver-shining hour
this moment in paved time
When my mother was born
in the heights of Algiers –
And before that
When her mother was born
into the lap
of Kabyle mountain land luxury
And my grandmother
when
her own mother of nobility name
was *Murabiteen* born.

Through instilled grace and inherited tragedy
And tattooed female faces tending to us in their
stoic way.
Endurance was not their first choice.
It was their only choice
And it painted homes in
Defiant, triumphant, joyous, eloquent yellow.

Some days I struggle to know what to do
with this heirloom of grace and power
as my generation continues the one before it
One generation moving forward for another
trying
maintaining
blistering
healing
present
in and through

one another
whether we consciously accept this sequence
or not.

All the lifetimes sift down
Like golden grains
to arrive
at my sisters and me.
I have no girls of my own though.
My son will have to learn how to inherit
a grand treasure chest
of North African women's heirlooms
Some adorned in solid silver and rare bright coral.
Some decorated in the strong songs of survival
Some are the sweet melodies
of ease and leisure
under silver green eucalyptus and olive trees.
May he have daughters.

The Scent of Goodbye

Goodbye or farewell
bislama
smells like
dismal cigarette smoke thinned out by
the cold wet air of a melancholy autumn drizzle
and the hot aroma of peanuts roasting
in an old tin basin
Above that fixture vendor's rusty old propane tank.
by the entrance of the darkened *Gare de St Charles*- in Oued Zerga, commune
Beni Bechir,
now Ramdane Djamel.

Middle uncle stood there leaning on an old pillar
Silently taking in
All our comings and goings of loading and unloading
crying amid frantic hugs
farewell
and hastily written addresses on scraps of paper
promises to stay connected.
The whole village seemed to come with us
wanting to say that sacred word
and tossing a traditional pail of water after the loved one travelling away.
They said it was a good omen to help summon them back.
We needed a sprinkle of looking forward too.
Grandpa was just buried
And grief polishes traditions until they shine.
Mortality and uncertainty stared us down
and we knew not to challenge.

But my uncle
did not utter anything at the train station that day.
let alone that anvil of a word.

His stare seemed to pull him
farther and farther away
From the scene
The gradual slow way a ship might pull away from shore
In a sad movie.
Maybe the long slow drag on the cigarette helped him inhale
Allowed room for
grief to burn him on the inside for all of us.
Because none of us could exhale.
They said he never smoked after that day.

We had no answers
for when the next hugs would be.
Did he sense in his still sadness
That it would be the last time he and I would meet?

Bold as a Feather

Small feather
Bold feather
From its protected home
deep in the crease
of a wing closest to
The core
closest
to the heart's timed beat
That began even before
the bird cracked
its brittle tough shell open.

Light feather
Fearless among heavier materials
Finding the mystery of flight
Through the whimsies and pulls
of different heedless winds.
A weightless small
curled floating feather
translates to metaphors:
To you – Beauty
To him – Chance
To her – Freedom
To us – Drifting
To them – Renewal
To me – Ponderings.

I ask myself with every one of the concrete possibilities of uncertainties
That all of us wrestle with:
What would I do
if my deepest feather escapes
and I find myself
On the wings of unknown winds?

How to be at home

Sometimes it means
cooking Mexican dried peppers pulsed into a sauce with
halal meat from the Palestinian butcher
who carries the best olive oil,
but will only sells you the best stuff
if you have a decent conversation with him
about how your Algerian family
kicked the French army's butt and are still separated from family across the border
in Oujda
Then the Pakistani uncle chimes in and tells us that's not too different
from what happened during partition.
We haggle over stories that remind us of the mirror we share.

Sometimes it tastes like Syrian shawarma in a hot bowl of Japanese ramen
Or an Ethiopian injera soaking up some Nihari leftovers that miraculously lasted
Longer than the Ramadan potluck iftar.

Sometimes it looks like
Wearing a *Kabyle* print dress
And waving a Chinese fold out fan at your face
to cool you down
When the wedding hall gets too full
Of the heavy breath of middle aged women
shaking their stellar hips and gold encircled wrists
To the latest Egyptian hit
At a wedding where the groom is from Libya and the bride is
Also Libyan
And Indian.
We know the singer is actually Lebanese
But music sounds more upbeat when it
Echoes off the pyramids
And the henna comes from the master Sudanese.

Tenacious

as marvelous dew drops
on knife thin reeds
or on a blade of grass.
water takes shape on sharp surfaces.
for a while.
Making light itself
Dance.

.

I get this picture in my round imagination.
As a child of survivors.

I do not need to share my metaphor during
the odd moment a powerful white woman
told me I should read
a (probably good) book
on resilience.
Aren't I standing here?
not just visible
but making life itself
a book?

To Boston

Goodbyes are heavy
Grease
Gravy.

They are most certainly not bright breakfast orange juice.

And most folk don't want to see the thick tears of parting.
They want to see some
Superficial easy joke
Some debonair laughter
Some hollow self-mirth
Some lighthearted evidence that you will not
give
The explosive releasing moment
Of a tear
a hot atom's moment.

Everyone seems too scared to stand that close to emotion.

But I will, because this city did that very thing for me – stood close.

I will embrace that tear.
Any other treatment would feel
unjust, hypocritical, short.

And I'll laugh again still
But not now
This choice is my luxury and my right.
And I mourn leaving you – old city.
Though you knew me only when I was unable to do more than kneel and
limp.
Your native trails cradled my fearful footsteps
Your ancient ground and your somber river waters
Helped me, held me up, pushed me
step by step back up
on my feet again.

Now Boston?
Goodbye.
And saying goodbye does not end anything.
It will only and always mean –
Now that you guard a piece of my flesh –
Thank you.

IV.

Grandma Gazes at Me Every Morning

Any morning
when I give myself a slip-fraction of a moment to really take a good look
at my few warmer memory snapshots.
My fresh dripping cheekbones after a quick ritual morning wash
outline my grandmother's face in the framed glass of my bathroom.

In that frozen moment I am reminded of a couple of yellowing photos she
refused to pose for but accepted to be captured in
between her tasks.

In one of them she sat with a plastic basin on the ground
by her slippered powerful feet.
The vegetable peels seemed to bow around her.
Her head is thrown back in a sad laugh
as if the photographer told a perfectly great dark Algerian joke
her small worn hands folded one over the other on her lap.

In one of the photos she smiles with tight lips. That's the one I see most.
Her small sharp eyes look down at the person behind the camera
but not down at the ground.
That's the one.

Her smile beyond the humid blur is framed
by two soft vertical lines
caressing the small space between and along my chin
all the way up to the corners
of my mouth.

I whisper her name.

When I miss them

When I miss my father
I spend time wandering pages
here and there
through my eclectic treasures of books.
Random wonder topics
Mind completely unfurled to the winds of curiosity and imagination.

When I miss my mother.
I speak in Algerian
And sing in Berber — or my attempt at Berber.
I look at my hands slowly—
fingers plump yet well-defined
fists softened and strengthened
by holding a pen and writing
by kneading
by pressing the ground lovingly
in prayer.

Mama's Words

You sometimes speak words
That dress me in a kind of ancestral armor
A power and rosy energy that make me feel
like I can move chest-forward
into the toughest life battle.
Do you realize the might of your ideas?
They are
the force of relentless water through dry cement.

Marching with Baba

Did I ever tell you that my father never
walked in a protest?
Never.
His scars reminded him too much.
The only exception was
when his Black brother, Brother Yusuf
school bus driver
Was killed one night on one of freeway 10's shoulders.
CHP officers dragged him out of his car, shot, killed him.
Matter of minutes.
Routine.
Routine traffic stop they said.
Routine cold blood we knew.
The men and women in hundreds marching around me felt like tall trees
protecting me and showing me how to stay standing.
I could sense their hot fear
I could hear their vast grief –
though there was a lot I could not yet understand.

Baba's hand tight around my wrist.
I can still hear his shout amid all the voices
"We demand! JUSTICE!"
Baba and I never exchanged words.
It was too serious of a moment
For me to interrupt him with my kid questions.
I understood from the energy of the stern strong gazes
That the most important thing to do right then
Was
to observe
to be
to demand and
participate
Keep marching.

Tell it

I want to beg her to share her story-
The one she dares not speak
Even to herself somedays.
I want her to shake herself by the arms
and then
RELEASE.
Release the pure incantation of
Tell your own story.

Do not stuff it down deep
under the blankets of fears and worries
Your
power
your
muscle and sinew
your
vigor and inner inner source
your source
Charge your surroundings with your magnetic narration.

Please

do not backdrop it to the stories of others

There's room for every one.

Please

Do not bury your story before it has completed its breaths.

Tell your story

Share it.

Rock it in your arms and hold it up to

the sun

the sky

all the elements and say

THIS

is my offering to you: my story-

hold onto it for its dear

time.

Being Right Where You Are

I imagined a conversation between the river and the bench.

"Good morning! Hello!"
The breathless river rushing, exclaimed,
As it always does
in messy swirls, hurried currents to the solid wooden park bench observing
quietly from the loving banks.
It greeted the bench daily, cheerily, longingly,
And "Good morning to you" the bench earnestly replied with its simple
welcome
And so their usual chat began once more.

"It must be lovely to be a river" the park bench sighed
mixed in its melodrama
"To come and go and see different places and people
and know that you can always be full.

It must be

Very very lively indeed.

Most of the time I'm on my own and cannot move at all."

The river splashed its disagreement swiftly as it responded

"Well, I on the other hand think it must be lovely to live as a park bench.

To know stillness and be able to daydream without carrying the weight of everyone

every single day back and forth.

It must be...." and her voice gurgled off,

leisurely.

Most of the time I cannot stop to wave."

"Well", observed a nearby bird,

"Do you not see, wild bench,

that you carry the weight of the walking folks

who stop for a rest or for a cry or a bite to eat or for a chat and a kiss?

They quickly come and then they quickly go.

With them you see

different stories and you move on to the next!"

"And you, thoughtful river", the bird cast its piercing glance out onto the stream.

"You move and move and spill along

yet you give a sense of pause to those who come to your arms

for a daydream to breathe in"

Both of you carry and both of you know stillness.

Both of you hold a place and a harmony with others, for others

By being

Right where you are.

Fog's Invitation

Hazy crazy
It spreads its zero syllabic roar over vision.
We call it fog.

It pulls its heavy cloak over anxious waters at twilight
thickening through midnight.
We call it "marine layer" in California.
We avoid sailing when it settles the low skies.

What, fog?
Can we meet and get to know you through conversation?

Impenetrable transparent
blurry mass
that won't be touched
and can't be grasped
nor bottled like sand and seashells in some nostalgic jar.

It makes peace with the dark and the dark appears to embrace it.

Could we embrace it too?
With all its mystery?

Maybe we're meant to sit that time out
let the fog visit and vanish
gentle and childish in its lavish and silky ambiance.

Fog,
If you were music
would you sound like a harp, a cymbal, a mystical flute of reed?

Fog, you pretend your force.

If you had power
You would leave some trace.

You position fear between our eyes and feet

planting seekers to the ground
Sluggishing every move
Heightening every sense

And then you part

evaporate

whimsically predictably

to show us we could see
if
we only draw close

to

what we wish to find
what we truly want to see.

What it's Like

Being a Muslim?
Imagine trying to find a quiet spot
amidst a relentless shrill
quick-fire clink clink clink clink,
slot-machine chorus of coins
deep in a
smokey-gut of a Vegas casino
trying to sip a call
that requires you to
hear your own
whisper.

Homage to a Cat Stevens song

It's not yet time
to walk away
release the pain
look out your window
You know there's more
so much more
so much more you want to do
And once upon your time you had much
Much you planned to do and get done
But when you saw high cliffs you wondered, dear God, am I all alone?
There must be some kind of shortcut
or at least a clearer trail
between here and over there.
Now you know
Now you see
Best to carve your own way
through those woods
Maya, Gwendolyn, Robert Frost
All made space from getting lost.

Make meaning out of direction
Don't let the daunted feeling swell
Trust that quiet inner compass
it still knows the way forward
well.

Daydream

Maybe our story will be like these two
Frightened and tall daffodil buds
braving the dead undergrowth
together
after a long winter.

Spring Morning

Some mornings
Gift us a peek into the tranquil idea of heaven.
The air itself
feels like it can't fit
into this smooth round jade and emerald planet
It's that massively beautiful.
Some mornings
The cup of coffee or tea grow cold after only one sip
Too majestic to miss while drinking
Too flawless
For human mistakes and pitfalls
Which we make anyway
As we toddle
Forward and backward and forward again
To the One.

AFTERWORD

It took a long time for me to accept the idea of publishing, even though my words conversed with pen and paper for years demanding to be let out into the world. This first collection, *Zmagria,* comes from a place of deep love— love for culture, love for poetic expression, love ultimately for this precious gift of writing. I hope that in this collection, my creative voice does not reflect only my voice—the voice of one *Zmagria* but rather the voice of every immigrant daughter, mother, aunt, grandmother, wife, and woman.

No one in my immediate or current extended family has published anything before, but they have all narrated a great deal within our family circles. Their narratives and voices have fueled my courage and imagination as I put together these works.

Zmagria is also my American jewelry box. I've happily assembled some of my favorite pieces in it, and each piece represents a unique cut, assembly, and arrangement of experiences, discoveries, and emotions. I didn't go about this in any planned way. The collection began with an attempt at telling parts of my own story. As in most chaos, though, an underlying pattern and order slowly emerged, one of a North African heritage, a Californian upbringing, and all the eclectic survival and surrender songs I collected along the way. There's not a chronology in these poems, but I did hope to capture some of the snapshots from different moments in my timeline up until now. While some poems reach for the surreal and can weave together images of moon bathing and local TV shows, ancient mythology and sports fashion in one work, this piece is decidedly about the real, the lived, and the angle from which I see life.

In my wildest dreams, this book would make you, the reader, curious about what I believe, about my Algeria, my Los Angeles—all of which conjure up some stock images and stereotypes, but all of which are far and away more than meets the eye.

Welcome, to my pages.

July 2024
Ann Arbor

A profound thanks to Zilka Joseph for dedicating hours to careful and caring editorial guidance.

This book would not be what it is without your perceptive and kind feedback.
Thank you.

ABOUT MOUNA AMMAR

Mouna Ammar is a mother, writer, independent scholar, researcher, educational linguist, postpartum doula, and wayward chef/baking dabbler residing in Ann Arbor by way of Los Angeles and Algiers. She has been writing since her early teens. Her favorite themes are love of the earth, strength, survival, spirit, and sustaining traditions. She derives her poetic inspirations from her North African culture and heritage as well as her Los Angeles upbringing. She draws inspiration from poets as eclectic as Alkhansaa and Langston Hughes, Allama Iqbal and Safia ElHillo, Al Mutanabbi and Aja Monet, Mahmoud Darwish and Sonia Sanchez, Pablo Neruda and Gwendolyn Brooks, Joy Harjo and Mary Oliver, Sylvia Plath and Suheir Hammad, Emily Dickinson and William Carlos Williams, Agha Shahid Ali and Hala Alyan, Janel Pineda and Amiri Baraka, Warsan Shire and Naomi Shihab Nye. This is Mouna's debut collection of poems and is only one beginning.